Mermaid things to make and do

Leonie Pratt

Designed and illustrated by
Katrina Fearn, Non Figg and Josephine Thompson

Additional illustration by
Erica Harrison, Katie Lovell, Jan McCafferty and Molly Sage

Edited by Fiona Watt

Steps illustrated by Stella Baggott
Photographs by Howard Allman and Edward Allwright

Contents

Mermaid paperchain	2	Handprinted mermaid	18
Octopus mobile	4	Mermaid mirror	20
Pretty shell purse	6	Mermaid pop-up card	22
Sitting mermaids	8	Coral garden	24
Striped fish chains	10	Sparkly mermaids	26
Underwater palace	12	Twinkly tiaras	28
Coral necklace	14	Whale riding	30
Watery bookmark	16	Stencilled shell paper	32
Sea horse pencil top	17		

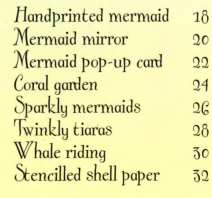

Mermaid paperchain

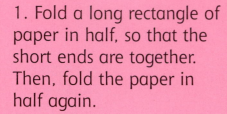

1. Fold a long rectangle of paper in half, so that the short ends are together. Then, fold the paper in half again.

2. Draw a mermaid's head and body. Then, draw her arms spread open so that her hands almost touch the edges of the paper.

3. Draw the mermaid's tail curving to one side. The tips of the tail should also almost touch the edge of the paper.

4. Draw a line around the mermaid. It should touch the edges of the paper by the hands and tail. Draw around the end of the tail.

Don't cut here.

Don't cut here.

5. Keeping the paper folded, cut along the line above the mermaid's arms and head. Don't cut around her hands.

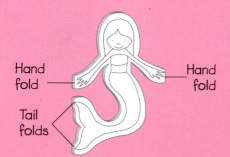

Hand fold

Hand fold

Tail folds

6. Cut along the lines around the arms and tail. Don't cut across the folds at the tips of the tail or by her hands.

Leave a white border around each mermaid.

7. Unfold the paper to make a chain. Draw three mermaids inside the other shapes. Then, use felt-tip pens to decorate them.

8. Use a silver or gold pen to draw scales on the tails and patterns on the tops. Add dots of glitter glue to some of the scales.

3

This mobile had an extra thread taped to the middle of the octopus' body after it was slotted together.

Octopus mobile

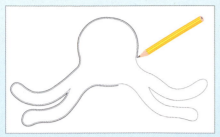

1. Draw an octopus with four legs on some cardboard. Cut it out, then draw around it on another piece of cardboard.

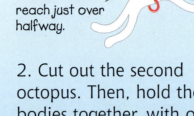

The slit should reach just over halfway.

2. Cut out the second octopus. Then, hold the bodies together, with one upside down. Cut a slit into both of the bodies.

3. Lay both bodies on some newspaper. Then, paint both sides of them with orange paint. Leave them to dry.

Splatter paint on both sides of each body.

4. Dip a dry paintbrush into blue paint. Then, flick your finger across the bristles to splatter lots of paint over the bodies.

5. On another piece of cardboard, draw lots of different fish to hang from the mobile. Then, cut out all the shapes.

You could tape more than one fish onto a thread.

6. Cut eight different lengths of thread. Then, tape the fish onto the thread with small pieces of sticky tape.

Paint over the tape, too.

7. Lay the fish on clean newspaper. Decorate both sides with bright paints and let the paint dry. Then, add faces with felt-tip pen.

8. Tape one thread onto each leg of the octopus. Then, paint blue rings along the bottom edge of each leg for the suckers.

9. Let the paint dry. Then, slot the slit of one body into the other slit. Draw a face and open the mobile. Add a thread for hanging.

Make a jewel for fastening by following steps 6-7 on page 15.

Pretty shell purse

Make the teardrop a little longer than your middle finger.

1. Draw a teardrop shape with long, straight sides on thick paper. Cut it out and draw around it four times. Cut out the shapes.

2. Hold one teardrop like this. Then, push the sides together to make it curved. Make all the teardrops curved in this way.

Don't press the teardrop flat.

Fold

3. Fold a large piece of thin cardboard in half and draw an oval on the fold. Tape one of the teardrops above the oval, like this.

4. Tape on the rest of the teardrops and draw a shell shape around them. Then, keeping the cardboard folded, cut out the shell.

Fold over any tissue paper that overlaps the edges.

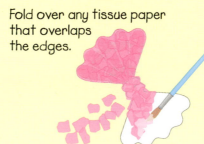

5. Rip lots of small pieces of tissue paper. Brush white glue over the shell and press on the paper, but don't squash the teardrops.

Put the strip to one side for step 8.

6. Lay the shell on a piece of paper. Draw around it and cut out the shape. Then, cut a strip of paper as long as the paper shell.

To make a clasp, tape on a small loop of ribbon in step 7, then glue a jewel on the front.

First fold the strip like this.

Then fold it like this.

7. Turn the cardboard shell over and tape on a piece of ribbon for the handle. Then, glue the paper shell on top.

8. Fold the strip in half along its length. Fold back one edge to meet the fold. Turn the strip over and fold back the other edge.

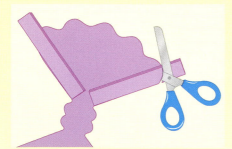

9. Cut the strip in half and glue the pieces in a V-shape on one half of the shell. Trim the ends of the strips to fit the shell.

10. Spread glue over the top layer of the folded strips. Then, fold the other side of the purse on top of the strips.

Shake off any excess glitter before you decorate the purse.

11. Brush white glue over the bumpy side of the purse and sprinkle glitter over it. Decorate the purse with sequins and beads.

Sitting mermaids

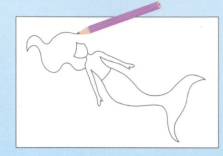

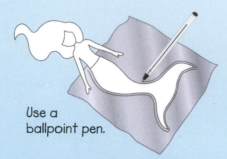

Use a ballpoint pen.

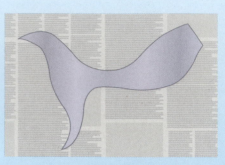

1. Draw a long shape for a mermaid's tail on a piece of thick paper. Draw a body, arms and head, then add her hair.

2. Cut out the mermaid. Lay her on the shiny side of some kitchen foil. Then, draw around her tail up to her waist.

3. Cut out the foil tail, cutting straight across at her waist. Lay the tail with the shiny side down on some old newspapers.

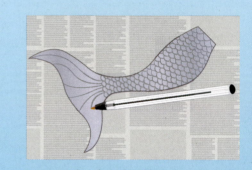

4. With the ballpoint pen, draw rows of scales to where the tail gets thinner. Then, draw lines on the fin at the end of her tail.

Glue the tail with the shiny side facing up.

5. Paint the mermaid's hair and body. When the paint is dry, add a face and a top. Then, glue the tail onto the mermaid.

6. Squeeze two blobs of white glue onto an old plate. Add a different shade of food dye or ink to each one and mix it in.

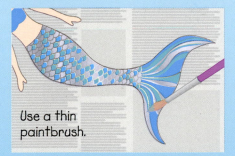

Use a thin paintbrush.

7. Use a paintbrush to dot the glue mixtures onto some of the scales. Paint stripes on the end of the tail and leave it to dry.

Bend the tail into a sitting position.

8. Place your thumb on her waist and bend the tail forward. Then, bend the middle of the tail back over your finger.

striped fish chains

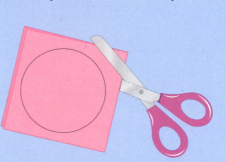

1. Rip different shades of tissue paper into thin strips. Then, lay a piece of white tissue paper on some plastic foodwrap.

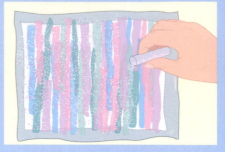

2. Brush white glue over the white tissue paper and press on the strips. Brush more glue over them, then sprinkle on a little glitter.

3. Fold a piece of paper in half. Place a mug on the paper and draw around it. Then, cut out the circle through both layers.

4. Holding the circles together, fold them in half. Draw the shape of half a fish against the fold, then cut it out.

5. Unfold both circles. Peel the striped tissue paper off the plastic foodwrap and glue one of the circles onto the tissue paper.

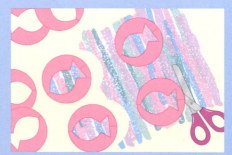

6. Repeat steps 3-5 three more times. Then, cut out all the circles that have been glued onto the tissue paper.

The ends of the ribbon should overlap the circles.

These chains were made using ideas from the 'Other shapes' box.

7. Lay four of the circles in a line with the striped side facing up. Then, cut three pieces of ribbon and lay them between the circles.

8. Tape the ribbon onto the circles. Cut another piece of ribbon for hanging and tape it onto the top circle.

9. Glue the other circles on top to hide the ribbon. Glue them so that the edges of the fish and the circles line up.

Other shapes

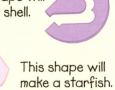

This shape will make a shell.

This shape will make a starfish.

To make an angel fish, cut out a shape like this.

Underwater palace

Draw shells on the door.

1. Draw an upside-down shell in the middle of a big piece of paper. Add a door with poles on either side, below the shell.

2. Draw four towers, two on each side of the door. Then, draw walls between the towers and add tall shells for turrets.

3. Draw curved steps below the door. Then, draw small shells around the bottom of the towers and on the walls.

4. Draw lots of mermaids around the palace. Draw their heads and hair first. Then, add the arms, bodies and tails.

5. Draw a sandy hill, then add lots of seaweed and fish. Then, fill in your drawing with watery paint and leave it to dry.

You could draw mermaids with different expressions.

6. Use different shades of felt-tip pens to draw over the pencil lines. Add more details to the picture, such as bubbles and fish.

These shells had
lines drawn on them
to decorate them.

13

Coral necklace

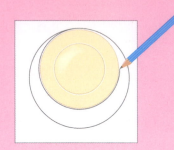

1. Draw around a small plate on thin white cardboard. Then, lay a saucer at the top of the circle and draw around it.

Overlap the edges of the circles a little.

2. Rip some pink tissue paper into small pieces. Brush white glue on the part between the circles and press on the paper.

Leave a gap at the top.

3. When the glue is dry, draw wavy lines along the edges of the two circles, like this. Then, cut out the necklace along these lines.

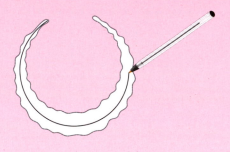

4. Turn the necklace over. Draw a line around the middle of the necklace with a ballpoint pen. Press hard as you draw.

You could use sequins to decorate your necklace, too.

14

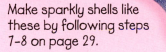

Make sparkly shells like these by following steps 7-8 on page 29.

5. Turn the necklace over. Then, pinch along the middle line, pushing the wavy edges together. This makes the necklace 3-D.

6. For a jewel, dip your fingers in white glue and roll a small piece of tissue paper into a ball between your fingers.

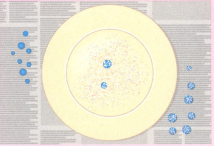

7. Sprinkle glitter onto an old plate and roll the jewel in the glitter. Make lots of jewels of different sizes, like this.

Glue the small jewels near the ends.

8. Brush white glue over the necklace and lightly sprinkle on some glitter. Then, glue on the jewels to decorate the necklace.

Watery bookmark

The mermaid's tail should bend to the right.

Don't use very dark pens.

1. On a piece of thick paper, draw a mermaid so that her tail is bending to one side, like this. Then, cut out the mermaid.

2. With felt-tip pens, draw scales on the tail. Leave a small gap between each one. Shade the end of the tail and fill in the scales.

Don't worry if her arms get wet.

3. Dip the mermaid's tail in a glass of water. Then, lean her against the glass, so that the ink runs to the end of her tail.

4. When the paper is dry, use a silver pen to draw around each scale. Use felt-tip pens to decorate her body and her hair, too.

Sea horse pencil top

Don't draw a tail.

1. Fold a piece of thick paper in half. Draw a sea horse's body, like this, then cut out the shape through both layers of paper.

This will be the tail.

2. Bend a pipe cleaner into a curved shape which follows the sea horse's body, like this. Then, tape the pipe cleaner in place.

Press around the edges until the glue dries.

3. Spread white glue over the paper and the pipe cleaner. Then, press the other sea horse on top and squeeze the edges together.

4. When the glue is dry, paint both sides of the sea horse's body and along its edges. Paint the pipe cleaner, too.

5. When the paint is dry, paint patterns and eyes on both sides of the sea horse. Then, wind the tail around the end of a pencil.

Make a sea horse charm like this one by curling the tail into a spiral.

You could give a sea horse to someone as a present.

Handprinted mermaid

Print the hair at the top of the paper.

1. Spread paint for the hair on a plate. Press your hand in the paint and press it on some paper. Do another print on top.

2. When the paint is dry, mix some paint for the skin. Fingerpaint around and around for a head, on top of the hair.

Drag your finger across the paper.

3. Fingerpaint the top of her body. Then, dip your finger in the paint again and paint two arms. Leave the paint to dry.

Keep your fingers together when you print it.

4. Turn the paper around. Press your hand in blue paint and do a handprint for the tail. The tail should overlap the body.

5. Press your three middle fingers into the paint and print them at the bottom of the tail. Then, make another print, like this.

6. When the paint is dry, fingerprint dots of bright blue paint onto the tail for scales. Print a row of green scales at the top, too.

7. Press your finger into some white paint and print two eyes. Let them dry, then use your little finger to dot blue on top.

8. Print small blue dots in the eyes and a pink dot for lips. When the paint is dry, use felt-tip pens to draw eyelashes and a mouth.

Fingerprint patterns onto the body, too.

9. Add some fish by fingerpainting around and around for the body. Then, fingerprint two dots for the tail.

Make a white
fingerprint on
top of a blue
one for a
bubble.

Decorate your
mermaid by
gluing sequins
onto her tail.

For a jellyfish,
fingerpaint a circle,
then add legs with the
side of your little finger.

19

Mermaid mirror

This is where the mirror will go.

You don't need these pieces.

1. Draw a big shell for the frame on the top half of a piece of cardboard. Then, draw a smaller shell inside it and add a handle.

2. Cut out the frame. To make the back of the mirror, draw around the frame on another piece of cardboard and cut it out.

3. To cut out the smaller shell, cut straight across the frame, like this. Then, cut out the small shell from both pieces.

Paint both sides.

4. Put the frame and the back on some newspaper and paint them. Paint around all the edges too, then leave them to dry.

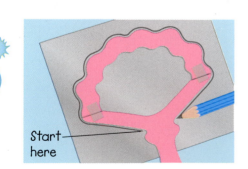

Start here

5. Tape the frame together, and lay it on the non-shiny side of some kitchen foil. Then, draw around the top of the frame.

20

6. Draw a line across the bottom of the shape. Then, cut out a shape for the mirror a little way inside the outline.

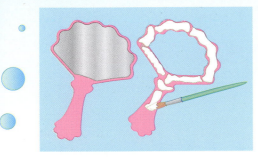

7. Glue the foil onto the back with the shiny side facing up. Spread glue on the frame and press it on top. Leave it to dry.

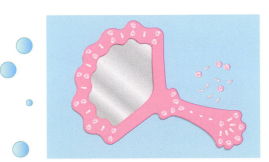

8. Glue sequins over the joins in the frame to hide them. Then, decorate the frame with more sequins and some beads.

You could draw a fish-shaped mirror, then paint stripes on the frame and add a sequin for an eye.

Mermaid pop-up card

1. Fold a piece of thick blue paper in half. Lay a large coin over the fold so that half of it is on the paper. Draw around it.

2. Draw more half-circles for waves along the fold. Leave a space between each wave. Then, cut them out through both layers.

3. Draw the mermaid's head, arms and the top of her body on a piece of paper. Then, cut out the shapes. Draw the face.

4. Glue the arms onto the back of the body. Turn the body over and glue on the head. Then, lay the head and body on shiny paper.

5. Draw a shape for the mermaid's hair on the shiny paper. Then, cut it out and glue the head onto the hair.

Try making
a long
card with
a swimming
mermaid.

Use a
different
shade of
shiny paper
for the tail.

6. Draw a tail and cut it out. Glue the tail onto the mermaid's body. Then, draw a top, cut it out and glue that on, too.

7. Draw a jellyfish and some fish on shiny paper. Cut them out, then use a felt-tip pen to add dots for their eyes.

8. Glue the mermaid onto the card so that her head is above the waves. Glue on the fish. Add the jellyfish and draw its tentacles.

Coral garden

Use different shades of green paper.

1. Rip a long piece of yellow tissue paper for the sand. Glue it along the bottom of a large piece of paper.

2. Glue another piece of tissue paper over part of the sand. Then, draw and cut out wavy shapes for seaweed. Glue them on.

Add tissue paper fish swimming around the coral.

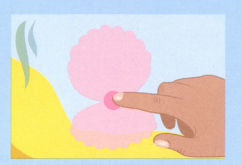

3. Draw an open shell on pale pink tissue paper. Cut it out and glue it on. Then, glue on a circle for a pearl in the middle.

4. Rip a large shape for a rock and glue it on. Then, rip smaller shapes for sponges and glue them onto the rock.

5. Cut some sausage shapes from tissue paper for a coral. Then, glue them onto the sand so that they overlap, like this.

You could glue a coral growing on the rock.

6. Rip more shapes for different kinds of coral and glue them on the sand. Add some small pieces, too.

7. Rip a shape for a turtle's shell and glue it on. Then, rip shapes for its head and flippers, and glue them around the shell.

8. When the glue is dry, draw outlines and patterns on the shapes using felt-tip pens. Draw patterns on the turtle's shell and add a face.

sparkly mermaids

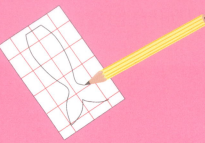

1. Cut a small rectangle of book covering film. Draw a shape for a mermaid's tail on the backing paper and cut it out.

Hold the end of the backing paper.

2. Sprinkle glitter onto a plate. Peel most of the backing paper from the end of the tail, then dip the sticky side in the glitter.

Fold the tail back from here.

3. Peel off all the backing paper and press the sticky end onto some paper. Fold the tail back, so that the glitter is at the front.

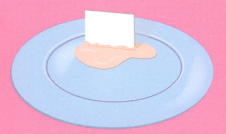

4. Mix paint for the skin on an old plate. Cut a small rectangle of thick cardboard and dip one long edge into the paint.

Twist this end a little as you drag it.

5. Place the edge of the cardboard next to the tail. Then, drag it a little way across the paper for the mermaid's body.

For a curved arm like the one above, bend the cardboard as you print it.

6. Dip the edge of the cardboard in the paint again and print two lines for arms. Fingerprint a circle for her head.

You'll need to dip your finger in the paint a few times.

7. When the paint is dry, spread some yellow paint onto the plate. Dip your little finger into the paint and fingerprint some hair.

Shake off any excess glitter.

8. Use a felt-tip pen to add a face. Then, brush a band of white glue for a bikini top and sprinkle glitter over it. Leave it to dry.

Twinkly tiaras

1. Cut a band of thin white cardboard that fits around your head. Cut a little off one end, as the tiara will sit on top of your head.

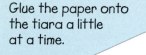
Glue the paper onto the tiara a little at a time.

2. Rip lots of tissue paper into small pieces. Then, brush white glue over the band and press on the paper. Leave it to dry.

3. Turn the band over, then draw a line along it. Draw a wide triangle in the middle of the line with its tip halfway up the band.

4. Draw a curly wave on the tip of the triangle. Then, draw smaller waves down both sides of the triangle, like this.

Cut along the bottom, too.

5. Cut out the tiara around the waves. Then, pressing hard with a ballpoint pen, draw a curve down the middle of each wave.

6. Turn the tiara over. To make the waves 3-D, pinch along the lines you have drawn. Brush glue over the tiara and sprinkle glitter on.

Make jewels like the ones on this green tiara by following steps 6-7 on page 15.

These tiaras had the back of the cardboard covered in tissue paper, too.

Press hard with a ballpoint pen as you draw the lines.

Slot it so that the ends are inside.

7. On thick paper, draw five lines in a star, then draw around it to make a starfish. Draw two more starfish and cut them out.

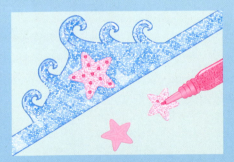

8. Turn the starfish over and pinch along each line. Decorate them with glitter and glitter glue. Then, glue the starfish onto the tiara.

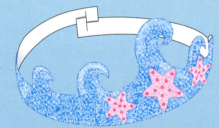

9. Make a small cut down into the band at one end of the tiara. Make a cut going up at the other end, then slot the ends together.

Whale riding

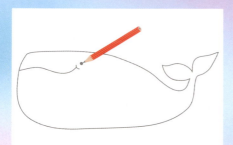

1. In pencil, lightly draw a large shape, like this, for the whale's body. Draw the tail curving up, then add a mouth and an eye.

The lines are shown in yellow so that you can see them.

2. Draw lots of lines along the whale's tummy with a white wax crayon. Add lines to the tail and circles on the body. Press hard.

The crayon will show through the paint.

3. Mix some blue paint with water to make it watery. Brush the paint over the top part of the whale's body and tail.

4. Mix green paint with water and paint the rest of the whale. When the paint is dry, go over the mouth and eye with a felt-tip pen.

5. On a different piece of paper, draw the outline of a mermaid's head and hair. Then, draw her arms, body and tail, too.

Make your whale spout water by drawing lines in wax crayon, then brushing paint over them.

The sea was made by drawing waves and fish in wax crayon, then brushing watery blue paint over it.

6. Use a wax crayon to draw wavy lines on the mermaid's hair and tail. Then, fill in the mermaid using watery paints.

7. When the paint is dry, paint the mermaid's top. Use a felt-tip pen to add a face. Then, make more mermaids in this way.

8. Cut around the whale and the mermaids. Then, glue the mermaids onto the whale so it looks as if they are riding on its back.

Stencilled shell paper

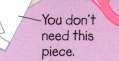

You don't need this piece.

1. To make a stencil, fold a piece of thick paper in half. Draw half a shell against the fold, then cut out the shape you have drawn.

2. Lay the stencil on a large piece of thin paper. Then, pour a little paint onto a plate and spread it out a little.

You could print small shells in between the larger ones.

This gift tag was printed on a small piece of folded paper.

Dip the sponge in the paint each time.

3. Dip a small sponge in the paint and dab it over part of the cut-out shell. Dab more paint on until it is filled with paint.

4. Gently lift the stencil off. Move the stencil and print lots more shells all over the paper. Leave the paint to dry.

5. Dip your finger in white paint and fingerprint a pearl at the bottom of each shell. Then, draw patterns with a gold pen.

Photographic manipulation: John Russell
This edition first published in 2014 by Usborne Publishing Ltd., Usborne House, 83-85 Saffron Hill, London, England. www.usborne.com
Copyright © 2014, 2005 Usborne Publishing Ltd. The name Usborne and the devices ♀ ☺ are Trade Marks of Usborne Publishing Ltd. All rights reserved.
No part of this publication may be reproduced, stored in a retrieval system, or transmitted in any form or by any means, electronic, mechanical, photocopying, recording or otherwise without the prior permission of the publisher. UE First published in America in 2014.